Cover:
The building designed by Frank O. Gehry has become a symbol of Bilbao, the city in the Basque Country.

1. Jim Dine, Three Red Spanish Venuses, *1997, polystyrene stretched over a steel framework, nylon mesh, red acrylic latex finish, three elements, each 762 cm high, Guggenheim Bilbao Museoa.*

The fruit of a collaborative venture between the Solomon R. Guggenheim Foundation and the Basque authorities, the Guggenheim Museum Bilbao has displayed its oustanding collections of modern and contemporary art since autumn 1997. And the setting in which the project planners chose to house them is equally remarkable: Frank O. Gehry's spectacular building moored to the banks of the River Nervión is now regarded as one the architectural jewels of the late 20th century. This special issue of *Connaissance des Arts* introduces the reader to the new Museum, the emblem of the changing face of the most important city in the Basque Country.

1

A
SUCCESSFUL
COLLABORATION

Preceding double page:
2. Built on a bend in the river, the Museum plays on all the site's constraints, in particular the La Salve Bridge, which Frank O. Gehry integrated into his architectural composition.

3. The building was designed to be an architectural masterpiece in its own right.

By Juan Ignacio Vidarte,
Director General of the Guggenheim Museum Bilbao.

The Guggenheim Museum has become an inseparable component of the contemporary Bilbao skyline. Yet, only a few years ago, the first models presented by the architect Frank O. Gehry elicted surprise and even bewilderment amongst those who imagined that that futuristic building would become a headquarters for one of the world's most important institutions of modern and comtemporary art, the prestigious Solomon R. Guggenheim Foundation.

Creating a European headquarters of the Foundation in Bilbao was one of a series of projects pursued by the Basque administration in order to help regenerate the economic fabric of the Basque country by diversifying the city's activities beyond its traditional industrial base, and, to contribute toward making metropolitan Bilbao a point of reference for the whole Atlantic region.

The idea that culture may be a factor in economic development was greeted by widespread skepticism and suspicion. Nonetheless, the popularity enjoyed by the Guggenheim Museum Bilbao in its first year has shown that culture can be an effective instrument to promote development and urban renewal, not to mention the support the Museum deserves in its own right, as a stimulus for creativity, artistic expression, and the promotion of a cultural identity. Our very positive experience proves that cultural initiatives can serve as potent developmental strategies, as they clearly help attract companies, promote cultural and business tourism, stimulate the service sector, and enhance the area's public image. Today, we can affirm that there is an explicit symbiotic relationship between a region's level of cultural activity and its potential for economic development.

The Guggenheim Museum Bilbao, which was always intended to be a unique experience based on specificity and not on duplication, has come into being thanks to the exceptional cooperation between the Basque administration and the Solomon R. Guggenheim Foundation, and on their complementary resources. The Basque administration provides its political and cultural authority and funding for the Museum's construction and operating expenses, while the Solomon R. Guggenheim Foundation contributes its collections, its special exhibition programs, and its experience in international management and administration. This is an example of collaboration based on mutual benefit and the need for each party to broaden the scope of its activities.

As a result of this cooperation, not only does the Guggenheim Museum Bilbao enjoy the privilege of being housed in one of the most outstanding architectural accomplishments of the 20th century, but it also has permanent, dynamic access to the fabulous collections of the Solomon R. Guggenheim Foundation. Thus, our Museum can devote itself to

4. The Museum houses nineteen galleries spread over three levels, around a vast central atrium.

5. Mark Rothko, Untitled, *1952, oil on canvas, 300 x 442.5 cm, Guggenheim Bilbao Museoa.*

gradually investing in artworks for its own, specific collection, which corresponds to and reinforces the spirit behind the shared collections.

At present, the Solomon R. Guggenheim Foundation manages three important museums: the Solomon R. Guggenheim Museum and its SoHo branch, both in New York, the Peggy Guggenheim Collection in Venice, and the more recent Deutsche Guggenheim Berlin in Germany. In this perspective, the Guggenheim Museum Bilbao will join the Guggenheim constellation, thus potentially becoming one of the most prominent international showcases for modern and contemporary art.

To achieve these goals, an essential prerequisite is an administrative framework that can guarantee effective

MARK ROTHKO

(Dvinsk, Russia, 1903–
New York, United States, 1970)
Mark Rothko is one of the leading figures in American Abstract Expressionism, a movement that attempted to merge form and emotion, focusing on the expression of the artist's personality. Rothko wanted his paintings to embody the universal nature of human aspiration through the use of large areas of color, prompting some critics to describe his work as "mystic." *Untitled*, 1952, is one of Rothko's largest paintings ever. It dates from an austere period in which all his compositions consisted of three horizontal rectangles of varying proportions, to which he applied a wide range of colors, combined in many different ways. The broad strips of color create a sensation of incorporeality. Rothko's painting has a feathery texture, giving its colors a nebulous, weightless quality. The rectangles seem to float away from the canvas and hover in the air before our very eyes. At times, Rothko superimposes several very thin layers of paint, allowing the lower layers to show through the upper ones, as if a hidden light source were projected from behind.

5

management of resources and international artistic excellence. Thus, the Museum's organizational chart is divided in two sections that answer directly to the Director General. One section encompasses Development and Communication, Administration and Finances (Finances, Visitors' Services, Security, Maintenance, Human Resources, Information Technology), Auxiliary Activities (Museum Store and Publications) and General Management (Legal Advisor and Administrative Coordinator). The other section, known as Museum Activities, is in turn sub-divided into Curatorship, Conservation, Registry and Education.

For this setup to provide maximum efficiency, the Guggenheim Museum Bilbao has adopted management methods aimed at optimizing program quality, visitor satisfaction, and private sector participation, in order to become a largely self-supporting institution. As we strive to meet high artistic and educational standards, support from individuals and the

4

business community is absolutely fundamental. It goes without saying that in order to attract new sponsorships, cultural institutions must be able to establish programs of incentives that satisfy the many participation, public relations and communication needs of these individuals and companies. The Guggenheim Museum Bilbao has therefore set up Individual Membership and Corporate Membership programs in various categories that offer a wide range of opportunities to our potential partners.

The Guggenheim Museum Bilbao has enjoyed an extraordinary and unprecedented level of support, both from society through the Individuals Members program, and from the business and institutional world through the Corporate Members program. Its inter-

6. *Prudencio Irazabal,* Untitled #767, *acrylic on canvas on wood, four panels, measuring 211 x 346 cm each, Guggenheim Bilbao Museoa.*

7. *Room 104–dubbed "the Fish" by the architect–photographed during the inaugural exhibition (19 October 1997), with the works of Robert Morris, Richard Serra and Lawrence Weiner in the foreground.*

PRUDENCIO |RAZABAL

(Puentelarrá, Basque Country, 1954)

Prudencio Irazabal, who lives and works in New York, is one of the most distinguished Basque artists of the 1980s. His work, considered post-minimalist because of its monochromatism, terseness, and apparent absence of the painter's hand, is a result of his meditations on the origin of painting and its various foretold deaths in the course of the century.

What immediately strikes us in *Untitled #767* is its bright and luminescent surface. Four different panels compose a single image in which the study of light and its transparencies suggest symbolic and metaphorical interpretations. Although the work appears at first sight to be monochromatic, on the sides can be seen thick superimposed layers of transparent acrylic paint that, like sediments, reveal the

6

action with society, as evidenced by the high number of visitors, is reinforced by the existence of approximately ten thousand individual members and the participation of around one hundred private companies and institutions that have made a substantial contribution to funding the Guggenheim Museum Bilbao's activities. Support from the private sector is particularly significant if one considers the innovative way the sector cooperates in museum management and the fact that such support extends beyond contributions to individual exhibitions, and is often on a multi-annual basis. In view of these positive results, it is clear that this original model, combining institutional support and private management, is proving to be an excellent management system for cultural undertakings.

process of creation. Thus, visitors can see the source of this enigmatic and deep light. Irazabal's painting is characterized by its "tri-dimensionality," whereby the sides are as important as the main surfaces. It calls into question the concept of painting itself, which, in the words of the artist, is nothing but "color, light and shadows aimed at the intellect and the emotion man has evolved in the presence of beauty."

J. I.V

7

FROM VENICE TO BILBAO

Preceding double page:
8. On the roadside, the public
gain access through an
entrance below street level,
as in an amphitheater.

9. Robert Motherwell, Phoenician
Red Studio, *acrylic and charcoal,*
218.4 x 487.6 cm, Guggenheim
Bilbao Museoa.

10. The Guggenheim Museum
Bilbao seen from across the
River Nervión, the city's veritable
thoroughfare.

Determined to anchor the development of Bilbao to the creation of a major cultural facility, the Basque authorities fulfilled all the requirements laid down by the Solomon R. Guggenheim Foundation, then on the lookout for a new site for its collections. Director Thomas Krens recalls the early stages of the project in an interview with Philip Jodidio.

Connaissance des Arts: You have said that the Guggenheim sought to expand because the New York and Venice facilities were not large enough to accommodate your collections. Why did you look toward Europe, and in particular to Bilbao, for expansion?

Thomas Krens: There was a long sequence of events. We didn't begin with Bilbao, but with Venice. We had a small position in Venice with the Peggy Guggenheim palazzo on the Grand Canal. There was an office and a staff, a program and a collection there. In 1988, I began looking at additional spaces in Venice. We looked at everything that was available, and we concluded that the only space that would have permitted us to operate in some relationship to New York, on the same scale, was another building on the Grand Canal, next to Santa Maria della Salute. We began a campaign that we are still involved in, to obtain a concession for that space. That situation there is complicated because the building is controlled by the Finance Ministry, but technically owned by a State agency called the Domanio. It is partially under control of the region and partially under control of the local government.

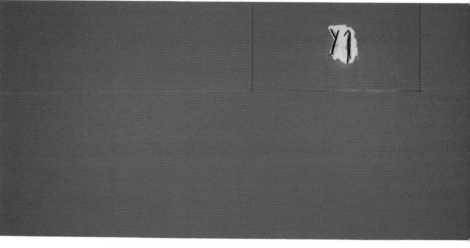

9

CdA: Your next involvement was with the city of Salzburg.

Thomas Krens: Our efforts to expand the Guggenheim in Venice generated a certain amount of press attention, and this came to the attention of a group of private citizens in Salzburg. My original objections to Salzburg were that it was too close to Venice, and that it is not a city of visual culture, but of musical culture. So we weren't interested intitialy. But in early 1989, when I saw Hans Hollein's proposed design for the project, our perspective changed in about thirty seconds. We began a lengthy involvement with the Austrian government at the federal, state and municipal levels. We completed a feasibility study in the summer of 1990 that was based in part on my experience at Mass MoCA (Massachusetts Museum of Contemporary Art). It looked like the possibility of going forward was very good. In my opinion, it is the collapse of the

10

*11. Frank O. Gehry's inventive-
ness can be seen in the design
and layout of the circulatory
spaces, as in the walkways
overlooking the atrium here.*

*12. Enmeshed in the urban fabric,
the Museum occupies the site
of a former industrial zone.*

*Following double page:
13. Room 208, during the
inaugural exhibition, with the
work specially commissioned
by the Museum, Sol LeWitt's*
Wall Drawing #831.

*14. The Museum offers several
different vistas of the city.*

Soviet Union that eventually stalled the project. It seems to me that the political will for the Salzburg project evaporated at that point.

CdA: What did you learn from your experiences in Venice and Salzburg?

Thomas Krens: By early 1991, the Guggenheim had refined its capacity to develop an international program. When you go through a complex planning process, as we did in both Venice and Salzburg, what you see is that there is a fundamental underlying rationale. It was not simply a question of using the collection more. There are numerous economies of scale with international operations. It doesn't take a rocket scientist to determine that we are living in a world that is becoming increasingly international or transnational. There are more and more projects that benefit from audiences in different locations. These conclusions were imbedded in the analyses that we did in Salzburg or in Venice. By that

12

time, it was a policy of the Guggenheim, adopted by its Board of Trustees, that it would explore relationships that could lead to this kind of conclusion. Our parameters for participation became very specific in terms of program, control and design – what we wanted from a museum.

CdA: You also came to reconsider the very nature of the art museum in the course of this process.

Thomas Krens: The very idea of this kind of international development represented a critique of the existing model of art museums. I have tended to say that art museums as we know them are a fairly recent phenomenon. The first public museums began to appear late in the 18th century. By the mid-20th century, it had become clear that museums could no longer be organized in an encyclopedic fashion. That was a valid idea in the 18th century when people traveled much less. In the

late 20th century, the diversification of audience, the ability to travel, the interests in specific histories or narratives fundamentally changed the very nature of the museum, and even of the spaces that it inhabited. By the late 1980s, it was clear that there was no longer any such thing as a "typical art museum." Much of the art created from the 1950s through the 1970s was already partially about transcending the physical limitations of the museum. Art first explored scale and expanded into the mind with conceptual art. It moved into physical space with the engagement of performance art, and from there beyond the boundaries of the museum and into the landscape, and back and forth. That fact raised fundamental questions about museums. It also seemed clear to me that over the long term, government operating support for culture was going to be declining, as more and more governments wanted to turn the

14

arts over to the private sector. New models of resource sharing would have to be created, and the development of any and all opportunities would have to be explored. The model of the museum that we had come to know and love was more or less obsolete. New things had to happen. The Guggenheim may well have been at the forefront of the analysis of these ideas at the time.

13

ROBERT RAUSCHENBERG

(Port Arthur, United States, 1925)

Robert Rauschenberg began to work on silk-screen painting in the early '60s. This technique makes it possible to scale images up or down, as opposed to other techniques which can only reproduce them in their original size. *Barge,* 1962-63, is one of the finest examples of this series of silk-screen paintings. As often is the case with Rauschenberg, it involves an overwhelming iconography culled from magazines, photographic archives, and photographs taken by the artist. He then asked a company to transfer the images to silk-screens of various sizes. On the basis of such works, whose subjects and techniques are derived from the mass media, critics at the time classified Rauschenberg as a pop artist. However, his work is a far cry from the cold,

CdA: How did you go from Salzburg to Bilbao?

Thomas Krens: When Salzburg stalled and Venice continued to make little progress, we began to look at other projects, in Japan for example. I also came to admire what Carmen Giménez had done in Madrid. There was an exhibition at the Reina Sofía Center of our permanent collection while we were closed for renovation. The publicity about what we were doing was so widespread that the question was raised as to whether we might not create a museum in Madrid, or elsewhere in Spain. It was in that spirit that Carmen Giménez organized a local advisory board. When I was in Madrid early in 1991 the suggestion was raised that

15

we might do something in Bilbao. Although my initial reaction was that Bilbao was not the center of Spanish cultural life, I accepted an invitation to go there in April 1991, fully expecting that I was simply being courteous with my hosts. What changed that situation was the determination of the local authorities. They knew they wanted a major cultural facility in Bilbao. They were making a substantial investment in the infrastructure of their city. Bilbao had been a city whose economy depended on steel and shipbuilding for most of the 20th century, and both of those industries were in decline. At the same time, the largest bank in Spain is the Banco Bilbao Vizcaya. The Basque region has one the highest per capita living standards in Spain. The Basques had also noted what had happened in Barcelona as the result of what might be called enlightened political leadership. Long before the Guggenheim was on the scene, the Basques had begun to launch five major projects for their city. There was the new subway line designed by Sir Norman Foster; a new airline terminal by Santiago Calatrava; a concert hall or convention center; a renovation of the train station with high-speed links to Paris and Madrid; and a new cultural facility. They had a plan for a museum and a location. The location was a city block in the center – a turn-of-the-century wine warehouse. It was a terrible location.

CdA: At that point you almost abandoned the idea.

serial production that characterizes pop art. His art is more a matter of gesture and of craftwork. It has greater expressive power, clearly visible in the hand-painted areas, in the collage-like superimposition of images, and in the intentional errors in the silk-screening process.

15. Robert Rauschenberg, Barge, *1962–63, oil and ink silk-screening on canvas, 202.9 x 980.4 cm, Guggenheim Bilbao Museoa, Bilbao, and the Solomon R. Guggenheim Foundation, New York.*

16. The Museum has welcomed nearly 1.4 million visitors in one year and has contributed to the development of tourism in the Basque Country. At the same time, for the people of Bilbao, the district has been revitalized.

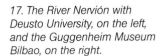
17. The River Nervión with
Deusto University, on the left,
and the Guggenheim Museum
Bilbao, on the right.

18. Room 306 with a work by
László Moholy-Nagy (A II, 1924,
oil on canvas, 115.8 x 136.5 cm,
Solomon R. Guggenheim
Museum, New York); in the right
foreground, a sculpture by Jean
Arp (Growth, marble, 80.3 cm,
Solomon R. Guggenheim
Museum, New York).

Thomas Krens: I said that it looked like it wasn't going to work. They asked me what it would take to build a museum. Not really determined to encourage them, I said, it would take six things. We would have to build a building, and the only kind of building that I could see being a success in Bilbao was a structure of spectacular architectural character. You can think of the Sydney Opera House, the Centre Pompidou–a building that was capable of carrying the identity of a place. I told them to think in terms of Chartres Cathedral. You want a building that would have roughly the same impact at the end of the 20th century that Chartres Cathedral had in the 14th or 15th century. I assumed that it would have to be a 35,000-square-meter building, that it would cost about $150 million, that they would have to build it, to own it, if we were to become partners. A subsidy would have to be provided that might be less than the

17

European norm but would still be considerable: in the range of eight to ten million dollars. We would use our collection, but as a sign of good faith and willingness to proceed, the Basques would have to provide a core collection of their own. I said that if they were willing to provide $50 million for such a collection, we would know that they were serious. I said that we were not interested in doing an architectural competition in the sense where you throw open the project and waste time. We would participate if there were three architects in a competition that lasted three weeks. We said that the government could appoint the architect, but that the Guggenheim would choose the three. We suggested Frank O. Gehry, Arata Isozaki and Coop Himmelblau–an American, an Asian and a European group would be the best choices. Each firm would be given $10,000, one site visit, three weeks and no requirements in terms of their presentation. The best idea for the site and the museum, and that would begin a two-year design period. The site would have to have prominence and distinction. I didn't really expect that they would do all of this. It was just conversation, but they did everything they said they were going to. □

18

HEART OF TITANIUM

*Preceding double page and
20. The building is composed
of several elements covered
in limestone, glass and titanium.*

*21. The different forms of the
Museum were modeled by
Frank O. Gehry assisted by the
computer program CATIA,
developed by the French firm,
Dassault, for fighter plane design.*

**Moored to the banks of the River Nervión, the great titanium flag-
ship designed by Frank O. Gehry is not only one of the symbols
of Bilbao's regeneration, but also one of the American architect's
most spectacular works. By Philip Jodidio.**

Thomas Krens, the Director of the Solomon R. Guggenheim Foundation, is
very clear about the ambitions he had for the architecture of the Guggenheim Museum Bilbao. He wanted a building equivalent in impact to
the Sydney Opera House, or to the Centre Georges Pompidou in Paris.
He wanted nothing less than an architectural triumph comparable to
Chartres Cathedral. It may be too early to judge its durability, but Frank O.
Gehry's great titanium vessel, moored to the banks of the River Nervión in
the heart of industrial Bilbao, must already be considered one of the major

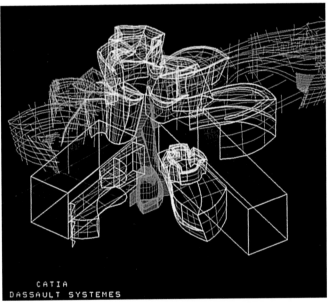

CATIA
DASSAULT SYSTEMES   21

buildings of the late 20th century. It is the new heart of a living city.
The visitor who comes to Bilbao for the first time may be surprised at the
location of the Guggenheim Museum Bilbao. A bridge crosses over the
Museum and it sits next to a rail yard. And yet, the location does possess
a surprising power. As Thomas Krens says, "It all depends on how you
calculate the difficulty of the site. For me, it was a kind of epiphany. On an
early visit to Bilbao, I went out for exercise, and I ran past the Museum
and across the bridge and turned past the front of the university and
down the side of the river to the old city where the opera-house was. I
realized that I had just crossed through what I called 'geo-cultural triangle'
of Bilbao. The site was right in the center of it. The bridge itself is interest-
ing. It was built tall enough for ocean-going boats to go under it and the
site was the location of a railhead. It was the former center of the shipping
industry in the late 19th and early 20th centuries. The river is really a

20

22. A panoramic view of the
Museum from Mount Artxanda.

23. The atrium opens onto
a terrace and a water garden
bordering the river.

deep-water estuary. Ocean-going vessels can come right into the city. The development of the city depended greatly on the river. Because of the size of the boats, the deep-water port is now out in the sea, but for most of the 20th century, it was on the river. The site of the Museum was the center of that activity. Not only for cultural, but for economic and social reasons as well, it was the *de facto* center of Bilbao. It seemed to me that the symbolism apparent in the location was spectacular. We wrote a requirement to use the bridge into the program for all three architects who competed: Arata Isozaki, Coop Himmelblau and Frank O. Gehry. Gehry's use of the bridge wasn't necessarily an architectural convention–it was a programmatic requirement. It seemed to us that there was a kind of final and fitting symbolism there–the Museum married the region by physically engaging the bridge."

22

The Guggenheim Museum Bilbao is without any doubt one of Frank O. Gehry's most spectacular architectural works. Here, the complex forms he has been studying and proposing for a number of years, for projects like the Disney Concert Hall in Los Angeles, come together in a symphony of sculptural volumes. The new structure has total floor space of 24,000 square meters with 10,600 square meters of exhibition area on three levels. From the outside, its most spectacular feature is the titanium cladding of its "metallic flower" shapes that were modeled by Gehry using the CATIA program developed by Dassault Aviation in France for fighter plane design. On the inside, visitors are greeted by a 55-meter-high atrium that cuts through the heart of the building. There are nineteen galleries, but the most spectacular of these by far is the main exhibition space which is free of structural columns and measures no less than

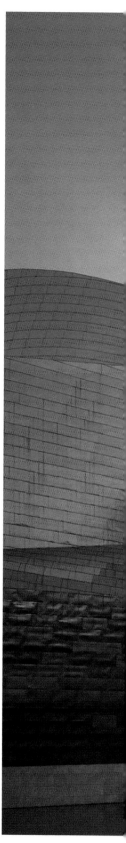

23

24. The veritable hub of the Museum, the atrium is over fifty meters high.

25. The Guggenheim Museum Bilbao seen from Iparraguirre Street, with Jeff Koons's Puppy *sitting in front of it.*

one hundred and thirty meters in length and thirty meters in width. Inevitably, such spaces do invite comparison to the cathedrals of another era. Gehry also reaches the apogee here of his natural tendency to want to create buildings that are in and of themselves works of art.

Born in 1929 in Toronto, Frank O. Gehry studied at the University of Southern California, Los Angeles (1949-51) and then at Harvard (1956-57). He created his own firm, Frank O. Gehry and Associates, Inc., in Los Angeles in 1962, but he was not to become well-known outside of a relatively small circle until almost twenty years later. The significance of his contribution was recognized when he received the 1989 Pritzker Prize, and in his acceptance speech, he described some of the factors which explain his style: "My artist friends, like Jasper Johns, Bob Rauschenberg, Ed Kienholz and Claes Oldenburg, were working with very inexpensive materials

25

–broken wood and paper–and they were making beauty. These were not superficial details, they were direct, and raised the question in my mind of what beauty was. I chose to use the craft available, and to work with craftsmen and make a virtue out of their limitations. Painting had an immediacy that I craved for in architecture. I explored the process of new construction materials to try giving feeling and spirit to form. In trying to find the essence of my own expression, I fantasized that I was an artist standing before a white canvas deciding what the first move should be."

Drawn toward the experimental freedom of artists, Frank O. Gehry installed a 1968 exhibition for his friend the painter Billy Al Bengston at the Los Angeles County Museum of Art using raw plywood, corrugated metal and exposed wooden joists. These were the materials that he was to employ in his first widely published project, his own house in Santa Monica (1978). Situated on 22nd Street, a quiet and not particularly wealthy stretch of private houses, the Gehry home, originally built in a style described as Dutch Colonial, was dramatically transformed by its owner, who added large protruding surfaces of chain-link fence and paved his kitchen with asphalt. In the early 1980s, Frank O. Gehry began to mark Los Angeles architecture in a profound way, albeit with relatively small structures. Much of this work was located in the neighboring beach-front communities of Santa Monica and Venice, which have since become a fertile ground for other leading designers. The Norton House (1982-84), a three-story residence built on a narrow beach-front lot facing the Venice boardwalk reflects the chaotic

24

26. On the floor, an installation in glass by Javier Pérez (Levitas, 1998, hand blown glass and mixed media, Guggenheim Bilbao Museoa) surrounds a work in steel by Susana Solano (Aqui estoy, steel and lead, 82 x 153 x 153 cm, Solomon R. Guggenheim Museum, New York).

27. As in all his other projects, Frank O. Gehry has designed some extremely original spaces, to which this view of the atrium bears witness. On the right, Soft Shuttlecock, by Claes Oldenburg and Coosje van Bruggen.

architecture of its environment, and calls on such varied materials as concrete block, glazed tile, stucco and wooden logs. In this very particular and ephemeral environment, Gehry has created a house that responds in an original way, and breaks the usual molds of contemporary architecture. On Main Street, the aptly named avenue that leads from Santa Monica to Venice, there are two larger Gehry buildings. The first of these, the Edgemar Development (1984-88), incorporates part of the re-clad facade of an existing dairy, and displays a remarkable variety of materials and forms. Five small structures, with three towers, clad in galvanized metal, gray stucco or chain-link mesh form a sculptural ensemble. The connection of Gehry's work to art becomes even more evident in the nearby Chiat/Day Main Street building (1986-91), where a central part of the facade is formed by an enormous pair of binoculars designed by

26

Gehry's friends Claes Oldenburg and Coosje van Bruggen.

Despite his substantial reputation in architectural circles, Gehry began only recently to build on a larger scale. His ambitious Disney Concert Hall in Los Angeles, located across Grand Avenue from Arata Isozaki's 1987 Museum of Contemporary Art, has yet to be completed. Gehry attributes this in part to the conservative stance of some decision-makers. "When I began to find my style," he says, "there simply wasn't much of a support system for anyone trying to do something different. Designers were kind of isolated in my day, and I found my community among artists rather than architects. In L.A., I've long been considered strange and odd, a maverick. For years, no big corporation or major developer gave me a commission of any size. Disney Hall, which I won in close competition with James Stirling, Hans Hollein and Gottfried Boehm, is

RICHARD SERRA

(San Francisco, United States, 1939)

The Californian artist Richard Serra, a master of post-minimalist sculpture and a close friend of Frank O. Gehry, expressed enthusiasm when shown the blueprints for the soaring space in which his work was to be housed. Serra described the gallery as "the great ship," which accurately reflected his perception of the room as an enormous protective environment for his *Snake*.

This work is made up of six winding steel plates, placed together on the floor, creating two narrow, curved corridors. They measure 31 meters long by four meters high and weigh 180 tons, but occupy less than one fourth of the gallery's total space. The complex interplay between the two creates a range of surprising effects, in which the spectator plays a decisive role; spectator movement and participation are indeed features that permeate all of Serra's work. In this case, the experiment, in the words of the artist, aims at reproducing a walk through the narrow streets of a medieval city.

the first big thing I've been given to do in my hometown. In Los Angeles, despite all its freedom to experiment, the avant-garde remains peripheral to the mainstream of most of what's being built. I think artistic expression is the juice that fuels our collective souls, that innovation and responding to desperate social needs are not exclusive imperatives." It seems unexpected that an architect with the inventive capacity of a Frank O. Gehry should build his real masterpiece so far from the "anything goes" climes of Southern California. This has to do with the persuasive powers of Thomas Krens, but also with the maturity of the Guggenheim Bilbao as a piece of architectural art. Gehry makes it clear that much of the program of the Museum must be attributed to Krens. Its spaces, from the atrium to the spectacular ground-floor exhibition room, and onto the somewhat more classical galleries above, were crafted with the idea that this would be no encyclopedic 19th-century-style museum. It is a museum for a new era in which people come to be entertained, or to discover the selected works of a limited number of artists. Art, when it is conceived in harmony with the space, like Richard Serra's powerful Corten steel *Snake,* sings in this space. This, it seems, is a place where art and architecture finally meet in harmonious amplification. In galleries used for large-scale paintings like those of Anselm Kiefer, there is another "epiphany," a discovery of what the art of the late 20th century is all about. It makes sense here as it never has in any converted 19th-century palazzo, or even in most of the purpose-built museums conceived in outdated modes.

The art within the walls of the Guggenheim Museum Bilbao will change. Its galleries were not designed with specific works in mind, and it has already received ancient Chinese art as readily as any contemporary painting. What will remain much longer is the architecture itself. A walk around the building reveals its true dimensions. What seems under one angle to be a jumble of incomprehensible forms resolves itself into the dynamic shape of an ocean-going vessel, an apt metaphor in this location. This, as Thomas Krens points out, is the nexus, the heart of Bilbao's history and development. The ships came in here and the city grew. With the hills and buildings rising around it, the Guggenheim Museum Bilbao takes on another metaphorical dimension that Gehry hints at in calling a "flower." The titanium petals of this rose are only the partially open heart of the flower. The rest of it is the city itself. The building not only "marries" the region by "physically engaging the bridge" in the words of Thomas Krens, it becomes a vital organ of the city itself. Bilbao unfolds from the arcing titanium surfaces of the Guggenheim Museum Bilbao, and clearly announces its intention to be a living city.   P.J.

28. Richard Serra, Snake, *1994-96, Corten steel, 401 x 3165 x 682 cm, Guggenheim Bilbao Museoa.*

28

THE SPIRIT
OF OUR TIMES

Preceding double page:
29. Visitors to the inaugural
exhibition admired the two-story
Sol LeWitt room from a sort
of belvedere.

30. Clyfford Still, Untitled, *1964,*
oil on canvas, 259 x 222 cm,
Guggenheim Bilbao Museoa.

31. Room 208 with works by
Eduardo Chillida installed
for a 1999 exhibition, Arco de
la libertad (Arch of Liberty, *1993,*
steel, 297 x 205 x 207 cm, private
collection), and Homenaje a
Calder (Homage to Calder, *1979,*
Corten steel, 190 x 222 x 170 cm,
Arango Collection, Madrid).

Seeking to convey "the spirit, the range and the exuberance" of modern and contemporary art, both the building and the collections of the Guggenheim Museum Bilbao break away from the traditional concept of a museum. By Lisa Dennison.

The challenge of creating a new museum and a permanent collection is a daunting one. The 19th century model, which has continued fairly un-challenged through the 20th century, maintains that a museum is located in a specific region, in a particular building, and is there to be a reflection of the cultural interest of that region or locality. The art is usually presented in neutral spaces (the famous white boxes of today's 20th-century galleries) where light can be controlled and little distracts from the experience of viewing the objects on display. Both the building and the collection of

30

the Guggenheim Museum Bilbao defy this model. The museum was designed with the intent to become an architectural masterpiece unlike any we have seen to date. And in his design for the museum, Gehry responded to a program that placed at the forefront the need to have new kinds of spaces in which to show contemporary art. How else can one explain the central atrium, fifty meters high and flooded with light from the glazed openings in the metallic flower that crowns it? This approach is equally evident in the boat-shaped gallery, dubbed "the Fish"

31

by the architect, which measures a hundred and thirty meters long and thirty meters wide. Free of structural columns, it gives the museum the capacity to present installations and works of art that could not be mounted in more conventional spaces.

In addition to being one of the largest contemporary art museums in the world today, the Guggenheim Museum Bilbao is exceptional in other respects. Through its alliance with the New York-based Solomon R. Guggenheim Foundation, the Bilbao museum is globally linked to the Guggenheim Museum in New York as well as the Peggy Guggenheim Collection in Venice and the Deutsche Guggenheim Berlin. This transcontinental network of museums allows the Guggenheim to develop collaborative projects and to promote international cultural exchange in a way that has no precedent in the art world. One of the hallmarks of the special relationship between the Guggenheim Foundation and the Guggenheim Museum Bilbao is the permanent collection. Founded in 1937 with a collection comprised of the most current and radical experiments in abstraction, the Guggenheim Museum has dedicated its mission to the perpetration and preservation of the avant-garde. Since its inception, the Guggenheim has continually expanded its collections, as well as programming activities, always remaining true to the utopian vision of its founding charter – that art, in its most expansive form, could truly effect change in the world.

The international vision of its founders has found realization in Bilbao's project, and in particular the aspects of collection-sharing that are at its core. The collection of the Guggenheim Museum Bilbao is being formed in concert with that of the Guggenheim Foundation, so that together they will reflect the full range of 20th-century visual culture. With the nucleus of the Guggenheim Foundation's collections providing both the aesthetic standard and the cultural/historical context, the Guggenheim Museum Bilbao collection will focus on the extraordinarily fertile period of art from 1945 to the present. The dialogue between America and Europe and the cross-fertilization of shared aesthetic sensibilities that have occurred throughout the 20th century will be an underlying theme of the permanent collection and exhibition program. As such, the identity of the Guggenheim Museum Bilbao will reflect the uniquely European/American axis that defines this collaboration.

The cornerstone of Bilbao's collection was laid in time for its opening in October 1997, and the inaugural exhibition was designed to showcase many of these new holdings. The acquisition program was shaped with several collection-building goals in mind, and fell into roughly four categories. The first is the concept of the masterpiece. Every great museum collection is known by signature works that come to be linked with the very identity of the institution. Therefore, one of the first priorities of the acquisition program was to find singular examples of great quality, and the curators turned to Abstract Expressionism, one of the defining

continues on page 45 32

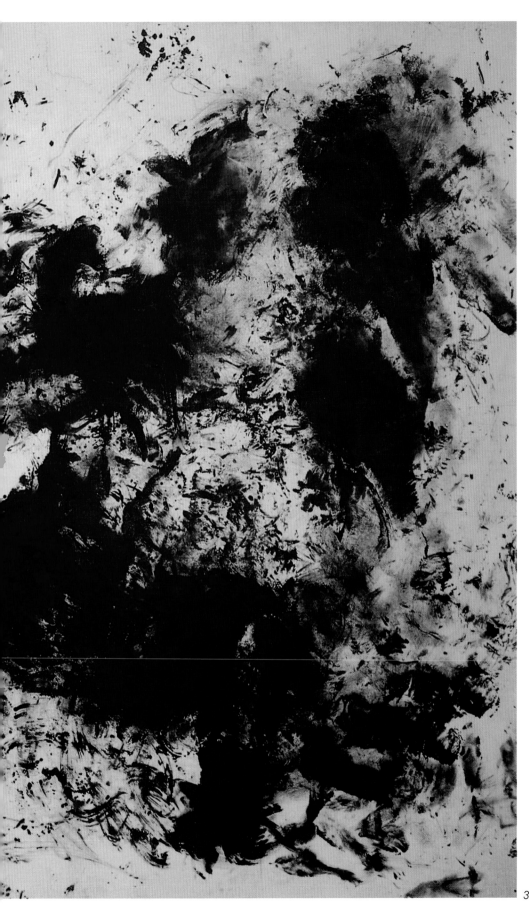

Preceding double page:
*32. A view of room 307. On
the left, a painting by Mark Rothko*
(Untitled) *and a work by Willem
de Kooning* (Untitled, *1952,
oil on canvas, 72.7 x 57.5 cm,
Guggenheim Bilbao Museoa); on
the right, works by Josef Albers*
(Homage to the Square: Appa-
rition, *1959, oil on Masonite,
120.6 x 120.6 cm, Solomon
R. Guggenheim Museum,
New York) and Robert Motherwell*
(Phœnician Red Studio, *1977,
acrylic and charcoal on canvas,
218.4 x 487.6 cm, Guggenheim
Bilbao Museoa).*

33. Yves Klein, La Grande
Anthropométrie bleue ANT 105
(Large Blue Anthropometry ANT
105), *1960, blue pigment and
synthetic resin on paper mounted
on canvas, 280 x 428 cm,
Guggenheim Bilbao Museoa.*

Following double page:
*34. Room 209 and the works of
Anselm Kiefer photographed
during the inaugural exhibition.*

35. Anselm Kiefer, Wege
der Weltweisheit: die
Hermannsschlacht (Roads to
World Wisdom: the Battle of
Hermann), *1982–83, xylograph,
emulsion, oil and collage on
canvas, 490 x 612 cm,
Guggenheim Bilbao Museoa.*

33

43

ANSELM KIEFER

(Donaueschingen, Germany, 1945)

Anselm Kiefer belongs to the school of German Neo-expressionism, marked by a return to the subjective heroism and brushstroke texture characteristic of German and Abstract Expressionism. Kiefer was born in 1945 in West Germany, a country scarred by the horrors of World War II. When Germany was reunified in 1991, Kiefer spent four years traveling throughout the world, before he settled down in France, where he currently lives and works.

The broad selection of Kiefer's work in the Museum's collection offers a comprehensive view of his artistic trajectory over the last fifteen years. It includes a variety of media–painting, sculpture and photography books–and materials–lead, straw, plaster, seeds, ash and earth. His works are often very large and virtually monochromatic; their monumentality enhances the solemnity and transcendental character of their content. Works such as *Roads to World Wisdom: the Battle of Hermann* reflect what until 1991 was his central concern: the history of his desolated homeland. To that end, he created a complex system of images that involve elements of Nordic myths and legends, esoteric philosophy, the history of World War II, and the works of the Jewish-Romanian poet Paul Clean. His most recent work, represented in our collection by works such as *Only Wind, Time and Sound* of 1997, indicate a new stage in Kiefer's career, with a new set of themes and references, free of the burden of history. His focal point is no longer man's external, but rather his internal, history, as part of a spiritual quest and an existential analysis of the human being.

movements in the development of postwar art. Abstract Expressionism not only put American art at the center of an international stage, but has wielded enormous influence on ensuing generations of artists around the world, both in terms of its adoption and its renunciation. The Bilbao collection has purchased signature works by three of the leading figures of this movement, Willem de Kooning, Mark Rothko, and Clyfford Still, whose works manifest the expressive gesture and lyrical color that are keynotes of this style. Another example of a singular masterpiece is Yves Klein's *Large Blue Anthropometry*, whose figurative and expressionistic impulse provides a counterpoint to his American counterparts. And finally,

35

significant in examples of recent works by artists with established international reputations such as Sigmar Polke were also being acquired in order to ensure the prominence and vitality of the contemporary collection. A second collection-building priority was to acquire in-depth holdings of a few individual artists. This methodology stems from the model of the New York museum, whose concentrated holdings of some of the foremost masters of the early 20th century, including Vassily Kandinsky and Paul Klee, draw people from all over the world to visit the museum. This biographical focus affords a depth of engagement that the encyclopedic collection is rarely able to obtain. Anselm Kiefer is one of the artists who has been selected to be represented in

34

a gallery dedicated to a grouping of his works that meld history, mythology, and literature. Spanning more than twenty years, the group encompasses all the media he has explored (woodcuts, books, sculpture, painting). Like the Guggenheim Museum in New York, the collection of the Guggenheim Museum Bilbao is housed in an architectural masterpiece. The innovative design and monumental scale of the Gehry building provides a provocative backdrop to the display of 20th-century art. Thus particular emphasis in exhibition programming has been placed on art that engages its architectural environment. In this respect, site-specific commissions are another focus of the acquisitions program. Jenny Holzer has transformed the soaring space of a first-floor gallery with vertical columns of L.E.D. signs. Since the mid-1970s, Holzer has used language, most often in the form of electronic signage, to express a wide spectrum of biases and beliefs, and here her texts are shown in Basque, English, and Spanish to underscore the universality of her critical visions.

Richard Serra was also commissioned to create a work that responds to the museum's heroic scale, and fulfilled this challenge with a powerful sculptural monument. Painting, too, can be made in response to its environment, and Italian artist Francesco Clemente created a cycle of seventeen paintings where the artist's visionary use of myth, allegory, alchemy, and rich palette evoke the narrative style of Italian Renaissance murals.

As a museum located in the Basque Country, the Guggenheim Museum Bilbao is building a collection of works by two of Spain's most distinguished living artists, Eduardo Chillida and Antoni Tàpies. The acquisition of works by a younger generation of Basque and Spanish artists also reflects an interest in expanding the collection to provide a more complete understanding of the significance and richness of contemporary art practices. The Guggenheim Museum Bilbao believes strongly in promoting local and regional artists. The inaugural exhibition was designed to highlight the newly created permanent collection of the Guggenheim Museum Bilbao. It did not attempt to present the 20th century from a traditional encyclopedic perspective, nor as a continuous tale. Rather, the nineteen galleries of the Guggenheim Museum Bilbao were installed as nineteen chapters, or short stories, on aspects of modern and contemporary art, the collective intent of which is to provide a sense of the spirit, the range, and the exuberance of 20th-century Western art history. Seen this way, the Bilbao galleries will have an infinite number of stories to tell. The potential for future growth is limitless as the museum takes its place as a major presence on the international cultural landscape.   L.D.

36. *Sigmar Polke,* Kathreiners Morgenlatte, *1980, mixed media, collage on paper and textile, 230 x 310 cm, Guggenheim Bilbao Museoa.*

37. *Jean-Michel Basquiat,* Moses and the Egyptians, *1982, oil and acrylic on canvas, 185 x 137 cm, Guggenheim Bilbao Museoa, gift of Bruno Bischofberger.*

36

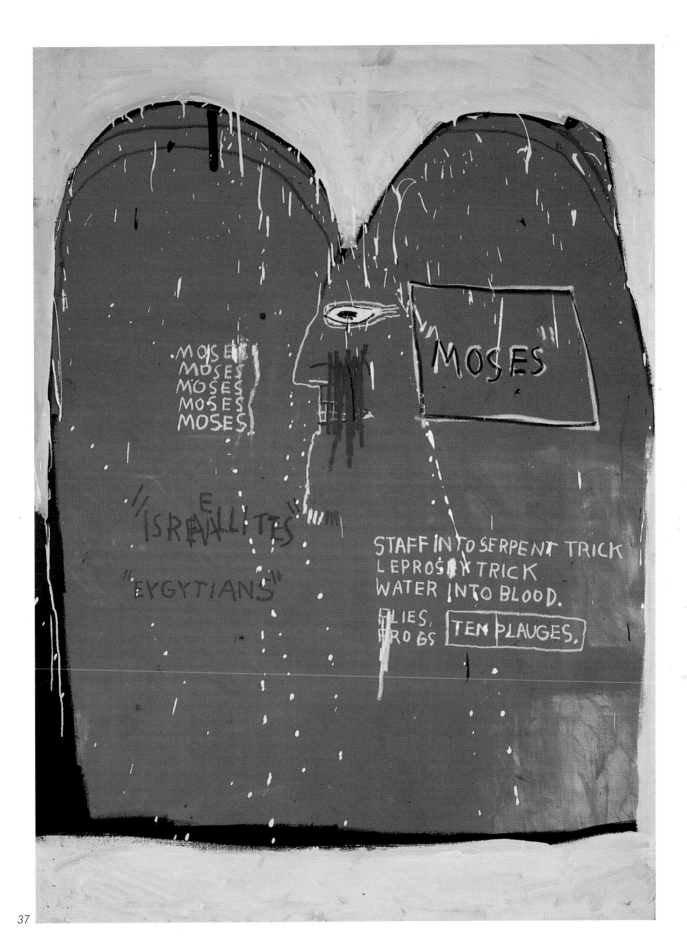

THE BIRTH
OF A
COLLECTION

Preceding double page:
38. These works from the Torqued Ellipses *series by Richard Serra were photographed in room 104 of the Guggenheim Bilbao, around the artist's sculpture* Snake *during Serra's 1999 show.*

39. Txomin Badiola, Complot de familia, Segunda versión *(Family Conspiracy, Mark 2), 1993-95, construction in wood, crystal, rope and photographs, 330 x 137 x 241 cm, Guggenheim Bilbao Museoa.*

40. Juan Luis Moraza, Extasis, Status, Estatua *(Ecstasy, Status, Statue) [detail], 1994, synthetic resin, 400 x 400 x 10 cm, Guggenheim Bilbao Museoa.*

Complementing the works from the Guggenheim Foundation, the Bilbao Museum's own collection comprises creations by leading artists of the second half of the 20th century, others specifically commissioned for the Museum, and works by contemporary Basque and Spanish artists. By the Curatorial Department of the Guggenheim Museum Bilbao.

The Guggenheim Museum Bilbao opened very recently, in October 1997, and yet certain distinctive features of its collection can already be identified. The underlying project has always been clear: to bring together a broad and representative set of modern and contemporary artworks of prime international significance. To that end, three specific factors guide our policy of acquisitions and lend them their definite character: the agreement between the Solomon R. Guggenheim Foundation of New York and the Guggenheim Museum Bilbao, the exceptional architectural merit of the Museum, and its geographical location in the heart of the Basque Country. These three criteria are evidenced by the approximately one hundred artworks in the Bilbao collection, the earliest of which dates from 1952–Mark Rothko's *Untitled*–and which can be broken down into three major categories: those complementary to the New York Guggenheim collection, those created specifically for the Bilbao Museum, and works by contemporary Basque and Spanish artists.

The agreement between the two institutions means that the Guggenheim Museum Bilbao may exhibit works from the inestimable collection of the New York museum as part of its own collection. Thus, one of the goals of our acquisitions policy is to aim at artists or periods in an artist's career that may complement and reinforce the New York collection. This group comprises both leading artists of the second half of the 20th century and other, younger creators who have achieved prominence in Western art. One can find major figures in abstract expressionism (Willem de Kooning, Robert Motherwell, Clyfford Still and Mark Rothko) and American pop art (Robert Rauschenberg, James Rosenquist and Andy Warhol). These American movements find their European counterparts in artists such as Yves Klein, Antoni Tàpies and Eduardo Chillida.

European artworks of the last few decades are also amply represented in our collection. The various media, techniques and materials that

40

39

MIQUEL BARCELÓ

(Felanitx, Spain, 1957)

characterize contemporary Western art are all present. An installation by Christian Boltanski or a photomontage by Gilbert and George mix with more traditional media such as paintings by Jean-Michel Basquiat, Enzo Cucchi or Julian Schnabel. For certain artists, such as Anselm Kiefer, the collection comprises a rich selection of works, bearing witness to their artistic trajectory and to the variety of media with which they have worked. Paintings, wood-cuts, books and a sculpture show the many facets of Kiefer's output. Following the path set out by the Solomon R. Guggenheim Foundation in its work with artists such as Vassily Kandinsky, the Guggenheim Museum Bilbao aspires to become an authoritative

Miquel Barceló is one of the most internationally renowned young Spanish artists. He divides his working time between Paris, Mallorca and Mali. The artist reinterprets traditional subjects (landscapes, still lifes, interiors) and autobiographical elements, which he represents on large-format media. He often uses materials that he finds on the work site, using techniques that confer an unmistakable texture on his works. Constant research, experimentation and innovation in composition, perspective, color, light, materials and textures characterize his art, in general. Barceló's periodic stays in Gao (Mali), beginning in the late 1980s, have had a clear influence on his life and work. As a result, he began placing greater emphasis on the

41

materials used, paradoxically creating a quasi-mystical quality that was previously absent. In the words of the artist, Africa signified freedom from a cultural heritage that had weighed heavy on his work. His subjects and artwork became much simpler, based on light, life and death.

Male and female goats, 1992, belongs to a series of paintings made in the early 1990s, depicting suspended or slaughtered animals. The work, reminiscent of the classical still lifes of Sánchez Cotán or the skinned animals of Rembrandt can be associated with animistic rituals.

center for comprehensive research on artists representative of the second half of the 20th century. The extraordinary power of Gehry's architectural masterpiece is also a direct influence: by virtue of the exceptional personality it confers upon the Guggenheim Museum Bilbao, it is a decisive factor in the choice of works that make up the second segment of our collection, deliberately chosen to stimulate a unique and fertile interaction with their specific environment. Art is thus drawn into a process of self-appraisal, in which spectators, architecture, paintings, sculptures and installations form a coherent, harmonic and ever-expanding whole. This phenomenon is evidenced by works such as *Installation for Bilbao* by Jenny Holzer, *Wall Drawing #831* by Sol LeWitt, *Snake* by Richard Serra, *Mother's Room* by Francesco Clemente, and *Cloud Installation* by Fujiko Nakaya.

41. Juan Muñoz, Sombra y boca (Shadow and Mouth), *1996, mixed media, polyester resin, pigment and motor, Guggenheim Bilbao Museoa.*

42. Miquel Barceló, Cabrit i Cabrida (Male and Female Goats), *1992, mixed media on canvas, 297 x 246 cm, Guggenheim Bilbao Museoa, gift of Bruno Bischofberger.*

42

CRISTINA IGLESIAS

(San Sebastián, Basque Country, Spain, 1956)

Cristina Iglesias is one of the best-known contemporary Basque artists on the international scene. The combination of industrial and organic materials, the large formats, and the varying compositions of her works beckon the visitor to walk around and sometimes through them. Iglesias also plays with additional information, placed deliberately to distract and divert the viewer from the perception of abstract form. Thus the introduction of details, such as exotic though identifiable flora, that can be considered narrative or representative.

Untitled (Jealousy II), 1997, resembles an exotic room or dwelling which, although apparently closed, can be entered. It evokes the shutters found on some Arab windows, which allow those inside–generally women–to look out without being seen. As in many of her works, Iglesias achieves seemingly antithetical goals: the room appears to be at once a refuge and a prison.

The panels making up the room were designed using complex, delicate and disconcerting geometric patterns. However, the geometry is fragmented and the designs are not what they appear at first sight. In some places, Spanish words and sentences may be glimpsed. According to Iglesias, this effect "is part of the mystery. I'm very interested in the different hidden meanings that we know are there but that we hardly perceive."

Finally, the Guggenheim Museum Bilbao is aware of its situation and its role in Basque and Spanish art. The Museum's collection includes such important figures as Txomin Badiola, Miquel Barceló, Cristina Iglesias, Prudencio Irazabal, Juan Muñoz, Juan Luis Moraza, Javier Pérez, Susana Solano, Francesc Torres, and Darío Urzay. In supporting emerging talents in young Basque and Spanish art, the Museum is aware of taking a calculated risk. It goes without saying that artists such as Barceló, Iglesias, Muñoz or Solano, just to name a few, are renowned nationally and internationally. Others, however remarkable (Moraza, Irazabal, Urzay), have just got off to a start, and the Guggenheim

43

Museum Bilbao lends them its confidence and support. In short, Bilbao's collection has from the outset been marked by its specific situation, at a propitious crossing of three roads. The Solomon R. Guggenheim's rich and valuable collection, along with its experience accumulated over the years, constituted a welcome starting-point for the new Bilbao collection. The Museum's commitment to the surrounding artistic community, and the privilege of being housed in such an architectural masterpiece, are the other factors that make for the distinctive character of this project. We are convinced that the future will bring further consolidation, as well as a readiness to take on the new artistic challenges of the coming century. □

43. Cristina Iglesias, Sin título (Celosía II) [Untitled (Jealousy II)], *1997, wood, resin and powdered bronze, 260 x 350 x 300 cm, Guggenheim Bilbao Museoa.*

44. Overall view of Room 303 photographed during the inaugural exhibition, with works by Julian Schnabel and Jean-Michel Basquiat.

44

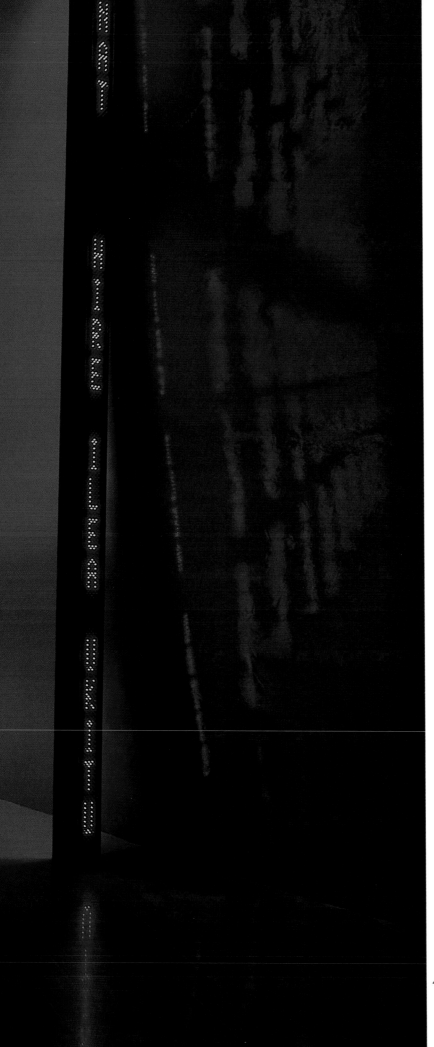

45. Jenny Holzer, Installation for Bilbao, *1997, light emitting diodes, site-specific dimensions, Guggenheim Bilbao Museoa.*

*Following double page:
46. Christian Boltanski,* Humans, *1994, photographs and lights, various dimensions, Guggenheim Bilbao Museoa.*

47. Room 105 with the works of Christian Boltanski, Gilbert and George, Jannis Kounellis and Mario Merz.

JENNY HOLZER

(Gallipolis, United States, 1950)
This installation by the American conceptual artist Jenny Holzer was designed and produced specifically for a room of the Guggenheim Museum Bilbao. The work consists of a series of illuminated LED columns of the sort generally used for advertising purposes. Holzer, however, uses this medium to transmit her disquieting messages to a trusting public, thus catching it off guard. In a museum, where one expects to see art rather than advertising, the effect is unexpected. The front of the work displays messages in English and Spanish, in red letters. However, on the other side, the messages, placed one meter away so that the visitors may move about between them, are in blue; moreover, they are written in Euskera, or Basque, although the content is the same. The "hidden" text symbolizes the relationship between Basque culture and the world at large. Holzer also worked directly on the surrounding space, painting the room's walls and ceiling in a bright gray that reflects and distorts the messages. This effect serves to enrich the work, extending it to fill the entire gallery and accentuating the contrast between the clear, straight letters and the apparently curved walls around.

45

CHRISTIAN BOLTANSKI

(Paris, France, 1944)

Christian Boltanski, one of the leading
contemporary French artists, became known
in 1986 for his magical installations of old
photographs, clothing or other personal items
exhibited as archival objects and traces of
individual lives. The spaces created by this
artist are reminiscent of small theatres
or churches, with their flickering lights and
shadows, provoking silent admiration
and a poignant feeling of absence and
loss. Boltanski's work evokes the salvaging
of the collective memory of peoples from
individual memory irremediably lost through
disaster and tragedy.

In *Humans* (1994), Boltanski uses photographs
of thousands of deceased Swiss. He took
none of the photographs; they rather come

46

from archives or the media, which underscores
their direct relation to reality. Our collective
unconscious assumes that since someone's
photograph exists, he must have as well.
Through his thousands of aged photographs,
the artist speaks to us of the death and
disappearance of the persons depicted, and,
at the same time, of the loss of identity. The
sheer quantity of individuals makes it impossible
to recognize anyone, to say anything about
anyone. Nonetheless, despite the loss of all
information regarding them, their photographs
remain, bearing witness to their existence.

47

GUGGENHEIM MUSEOAK ETA
MENDE HONETAKO ARTEA

LOS MUSEOS GUGGENHEIM
Y EL ARTE DE ESTE SIGLO

THE GUGGENHEIM MUSEUMS
AND THE ART OF THIS CENTURY

Guggenheim Bilbao Museoa

Preceding double page:
48. The Museum is part of the urban regeneration scheme launched by Bilbao in 1989, which includes a convention center, an international airport designed by Santiago Calatrava, a new subway station designed by Sir Norman Foster and a renovation program for the banks of the Nervión undertaken by Cesar Pelli.

49. The entrance to the auditorium and the staircase leading down to the river.

50. Plans of the first, second and third floors.

Guggenheim Museum Bilbao, avenida Abandoibarra 2, 48001 Bilbao. Telephone: (34) 94-4359080. Fax: (34) 94-4359040.

Visiting Hours. The Museum is opened from Tuesday to Sunday, 10 am to 8 pm. Closed Monday. Ticket sales end thirty minutes prior to closing

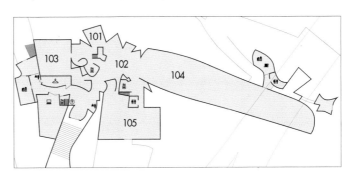

50

time. The exhibition rooms begin to close at 7.45 pm.

Admission fees. Adults: 800 pesetas/4.81 euros. Students: 400 pesetas/ 2.40 euros. Senior Citizens: 400 pesetas/2.40 euros. Children under 12: free. Groups (over 20 people): 600 pesetas/3.61 euros. The admission fee is valid the entire day, with the right to exit and enter freely.

Visitor Information. There is an information counter in the lobby, where visitors may make queries. A free guidebook to the Museum is also available, *@Guggenheim,* containing information on current exhibitions and schedules of guided tours, lectures, etc., both for Individuals Members of the Museum and for the public at large.

Free guided tours. The Guggenheim Museum Bilbao offers free daily

49

51. Julian Schnabel, España (Spain), 1986, oil, plates and Bondo on wood, 333 x 513 cm, Guggenheim Bilbao Museoa.

52. View of the atrium from the second floor of the Museum.

guided tours. For schedule information, call 94-435 90 80 during visiting hours. Groups may register 30 minutes prior to each tour at the information counter.

Special guided tours. Special tours are also available on request. Prior booking is required. They are given by art professionals specialized in the permanent collection, the temporary exhibitions and the Museum's architecture. Information and bookings Monday-Friday from 9 am to 2 pm. Telephone: 94-435 90 90. Fax: 94-435 90 39.

Groups. A special group entrance is located in the riverside facade. Groups of over 20 must give advanced notification so that the Visitor Services Department may organize the visit. Information may be obtained Monday-Friday from 9 am to 2 pm at 94-435 90 23.

Facilities for the handicapped. The Museum has special elevators

51

and ramps for the handicapped. A ramp is also available at the group entrance, in the riverside facade.

Special programs. The Individual Member program offers a wide range of advantages and activities. Subscription charges vary according to membership category (student, over-65, individual, family or international member). For further information, call: 94-435 90 14. There is also a "Corporate Membership" program for companies and institutions interested in participating in the Museum's development. For further information, call: 94-435 90 16.

Educational activities. Visits and workshops for primary school and kindergarten groups, guided tours for secondary education students

52